The Surname Barrett

Susan Morris &
Wendy Bosberry-Scott

ISBN: 10: 1535552611
ISBN-13: 978-1535552615

The question of surnames, their origins, distribution and history, lies at the heart of genealogy as well as being fascinating in its own right.

In the 1980s and 1990s, long before many genealogical sources were even indexed, let alone online, our Surname Report service provided expert assessments of the origins, history and distribution of selected British surnames, using the sources available at the time.

Now, with so many more sources available, we believe that these reports retain their value as studies of individual surnames, and so we are gradually making the Debrett Surname Archive available online and in print for the first time. Some modern indexes have been consulted to refresh and update the reports.

Debrett Ancestry Research Ltd, PO Box 379,
Winchester SO23 9YQ
Tel: 01962 841904
Email: info@debrettancestry.co.uk
Website: www.debrettancestry.co.uk

CONTENTS

Overview   1

Origins   3

Distribution   7

Famous Bearers of the Name   23

Printed Genealogies   28

Summary   31

Sources Consulted   32

Overview

The use of surnames in England began in the Norman period, when surnames were not necessarily hereditary but usually a form of description. Some described the individual's trade or profession; others were nicknames; some gave the father's Christian name; others gave the individual's place of residence or origin.

Different surnames might be used in different documents, or more than one surname given in one document. Early descriptions were fairly elaborate and by the thirteenth and fourteenth centuries these were simpler, but still variable, and indeed the instability of surnames continued until well into the seventeenth century.

Although some Normans would already have had hereditary surnames on their arrival in Britain, the passing on of a surname from generation to generation only became customary in Britain gradually during the course of the thirteenth and fourteenth centuries. At the end of this period most of the population apparently had surnames.

Variations in the spelling of a family's surname continue to be found until the present century. Before this, as most people could not read or write, the parish clerk or other official would write down the name as they heard it.

There are four main groups of surnames:

A – Local names, which describe a person by his place of residence or origin.

B – Occupational names, which describe a person by his trade or profession.

C – Surnames of relationship, which refer to the Christian name of the father or other important relative.

D – Nicknames or sobriquets, coined to describe a person in terms of his appearance or character.

Many surnames have uncertain origins, and as we will see, Barrett (which in this report is treated together with its variants Barrat, Barratt, Barritt and Barrott) could fall into Category B, C or D.

Origins

The *Patronymica Brittanica,* an early but still interesting surname dictionary (1860), gives Barratt and Barrett separate entries:

> **Barratt**
> The same as Barrett, which see. One family so called settled in England on the persecution of the Fr[ench] Protestants, consequent upon the Revocation of the Edict of Nantes.

> **Barrett, Barritt, &c**
> Barets, a personal name of Teutonic origin, is found here in Saxon times. See Domesd[ay]. In various forms it has always been very common in France and England.

Charles W Bardsley, in his *Dictionary of English and Welsh Surnames (with special American Instances)* (1901), describes Barrett (as part of the group Barrat(t), Barret(t), Berret(t)) as 'a great surname', noting that it appears (as Baret) as a personal name in the Domesday Book in Yorkshire. He found three examples of Barat or Baret as a surname in the Hundred Rolls of 1273:

> Agnes Barat, Cambridgeshire
> Harvey Baret, Norfolk
> John Baret, Lincolnshire

Bardsley links the name Barat/Baret with the personal names Berold and (French) Beraud, and he also notes two early examples of these in English records:

> Stephanus fil[ius] Beroldi, Pipe Rolls, 5 Henry II [1158/9]
> Berard de Wattlesfeld, Suffolk, Hundred Rolls, 1273

However, P H Reaney and R M Wilson's entry in the authoritative *Dictionary of English Surnames* (Oxford, 1995: effectively a third edition of P H Reaney's *A Dictionary of British Surnames*, 1958) present a more complex picture. They too noted Stephanus *filius* Beroldi (Stephen son of Berold) but regard both Berold and Berard as separate given names, which have both given rise to their own surnames (Berald/Beraud and Berard). Their entry for Barrett (etc) reads as follows:

> **Barrat, Barratt, Barrett, Barritt, Barrott**
> This is a difficult name. There seems no evidence for a derivation from OG [Old German] *Beroald*, OFr [Old French] *Beraud*, as has been suggested. ON [Old Norse] *Bárðr* is found in Yorks and Lincs in DB [Domesday Book] as *Bared, Baret*, but there is no proof of its continued use.
>
> The commonest form is *Barat* and this must be from OFr *barat*, ME [Middle English] *bar(r)at, bar(r)et(te)*, which accounts for all the forms. The original sense in Romanic seems to have been 'traffic, commerce, dealing', and in ME 'trouble, distress' (c1230); 'deception, fraud' (1292); 'contention, strife' (c1300), from any of which a nickname could arise. Occasionally we may have OFr *barrette* 'a cap, bonnet', as an occupation name, 'a maker of caps'.

4

Thus Reaney and Wilson not only differentiated the Bar(r)at(t)/Bar(r)et(t) group from Berold and Beraud (*etc*) but also disconnected it from the Domesday personal name Baret (or Bared), which they suggested had a Nordic origin. They put forward the new suggestion that most likely source of the surname Bar(r)at(t)/Bar(r)et(t) was the old French word *barat*, which in the Romanic or Romance languages originally meant 'traffic, commerce, dealing'. From this evolved the Middle English words *bar(r)at and bar(r)et(te)* meaning 'trouble, distress' at the beginning of the thirteenth century which later came to mean 'deception, fraud, contention, strife'. The surname might therefore have arisen as a nickname for someone involved in commerce or with the negative associations that became attached to the word in Middle English. Finally, they throw in the suggestion that some forms of the surname may have derived from the old French word for cap or bonnet and could therefore denote someone who was a maker of caps, which would put the surname Barrett into the category of occupational names.

The earliest examples Reaney and Wilson found for this surname are as follows:

ca1150-5	Matthew Baret [Lincolnshire]: F M Stenton *Documents illustrative of the Social and Economic History of the Danelaw* (London, 1920)
1165	Robert Barate – Pipe Rolls, Nottinghamshire

1185	Jordan Barat [Hertfordshire]: B A Lees, *Records of the Templars in England in the Twelfth Century* (London, 1935)
1207	Seman Barette – Pipe Rolls, Hampshire
1327	William Barrett – Subsidy Rolls, Essex [also found as William Baratt]

This list shows a fairly wide spread of examples in Lincolnshire, Nottinghamshire, London, Hampshire and Essex, and none of them appears in a form that would suggest a personal name origin.

Patrick Hank and Flavia Hodges' *Dictionary of Surnames* (Oxford 1988) has a wider geographical scope but gives a looser discussion of each surname, citing no examples. Hank and Hodges adopt Reaney's findings on the Middle English word *bar(r)et(t)e* or *bar(r)at*, noting its derivation from the Old French verb *barater,* meaning to barter or haggle. They note further that Italian cognates preserve the original sense of a market trader, without the negative connotations. They are however less particular than Reaney in putting forward the alternative theories of a personal name origin and of a connection with the Old French word for a cap or bonnet, *barette,* which they suggest might have given rise to a nickname as well as being a possibly occupational name.

Distribution

The only volume of the English Surnames Series (which is very incomplete) to mention the surname Barrett *etc*, is that for the West Riding of Yorkshire, the first volume in the series (George Redmonds, 1973). The author of this work assumes that the surname Barrett, which he describes as a West Riding surname, is derived from the personal name Baret, and he notes that the nickname 'Barehead' 'was probably absorbed by Barrett' (page 10). The name Barrett was found in the 1379 Poll Tax returns in Farnhill and Steeton, which lie between Skipton and Keighley, and by 1560 in Gargrave, which lies just north west of Skipton.

The published *Calendar to the Feet of Fines for London and Middlesex 1189-1485* includes a single reference to the surname Baret. (The fine was a means of conveying or settling freehold property.)

> **Edward 1 Anno 34 (1306)**
> John Baret and Alice his wife and William de Insula. A messuage in Westminster

This shows that in 1306 John and Alice Baret were parties to the sale of a messuage (a house and the ground around it) in Westminster. In H R Moulton's *Palaeography, Genealogy and Topography*, primarily a sale catalogue printed in the 1930s listing historical documents, ancient charters, leases, court rolls *etc.*, there were several entries for variants of the name Barrett *etc*:

5 May 1322
Grant by Sir William le Blount, knight, lord of Belton in Rotelond, to Simon le Swonde, Attheloxshton and Maud his wife for their lives, of a cottage with the buildings thereon standing in Belton, which John son of Roger held of the grantor, lying between the messuage of Richard the Shepherd and that which William son of the widow holds of the grantor in villeinage, at a yearly rent of 2s. Witnesses: Walter de Belton, William Cok of the same, Nicholas le Freyne of the same, John son of Philip of the same, John Baret of the same. Belton. Wednesday after the Invention of the Cross 15 Edward II. – £6

18 July 1561
Feoffment by Thomas Spyer, the younger, son of Ralph Spyer, late of Mares, County Oxfordshire, yeoman, deceased, to Thomas Spyer, the elder of Tuffield, County Oxfordshire, yeoman of all lands called Pottye otherwise Potters in Benson otherwise Bensyngton, County Oxfordshire. Witnesses: William Mercer, Ralph Spyer, Geoffey Barrett, William Huntley. – 25/-

3 April 1588
Grant by Andrew Barrate of Burnbie on the More, County Nottinghamshire, to William Clarke, labourer, of Lownde juxta Sutton, County Nottinghamshire, of a toft in Burnbie aforesaid. Seal. – 20/-

3 November 1595
Lease. Marchan. 50 years. Bessells Fetiplace of Beselslight, county Berkshire and Richard Fetiplace his son to Richard White of Marcham, county Berkshire,

Marian his wife, Elizabeth White, their daughter. Witnesses: Lawrence Whistler, George Newmans, John Wirdnain, Thomas Barrett. Signatures: Besells Fetiplace, Richard Fetiplace. Fragment of seal. – 30/-

27 April 1610
Indenture of bargain and sale by William Barrett of Whitley in Wootton Warren, county Warwickshire, yeoman, Margaret his wife, and John their son, of the one part, to Thomas Troute of Studley, county Warwickshire, yeoman of the other part, of a cottage and lands in Allenhall in Wootton Warren, county Warwickshire. Witnesses: Thomas Warner, Nicholas Knight, mark of Richard Bourton, Willyam Trent. Signatures: William Bassett, John Baret – 15/-

13 March 1630
Lease by Sir William Russell of Strensham, Bart., and Edward Barrett of Droitwich, to George, Earl of Shrewsbury, of a house called Batchcoates, in Cooksey, County Worcestershire. – £1/5/-

3 October 1661
Release. Wisborough Green. Alice Francis of Wisborough Green, county Sussex to Dorothy Barrett of Witley, county Surrey, spinster. Witnesses: Edmond Yalden, Henry Harden, George Shadd. Signature of Alles Fruces. Armorial Seal. – 25/-

31 January 1671
Indenture, being a mortgage by William Barrett, yeoman, of Godmanchester, county Huntingdonshire, to John Manning, citizen of London, of the reversion which the said William has in a messuage or tenement

in Newsells and land in Backway and Reed, county Hertfordshire. Signature of mortgagee. – 10/6

Willoughby of Parham and Molineux of Hawkley. Roll pedigree of the family of Hugh, Lord Willoughby of Parham from Sir John Willoughby, a Norman Knight – arms supporters and quartering tricked in colour, 17 coats. Also a pedigree of the family of Molineux of Hawkley. Arms tricked in colour. Both pedigrees copied from Barritt's Lancashire Pedigrees in the Chetham College Library by Richard Heming of Ardwick Manchester in 1874. – £2

These documents show that various forms of the surname had spread over a wide area of England by the sixteenth and seventeenth centuries.

In 1890 H B Guppy published his *Homes of Family Names in Great Britain*, still the only published work on surname distribution in Britain as a whole. His work was based on printed genealogies and a survey of county directories for the 1880s, in which he looked especially at the names of farmers, reasoning that they were among the most stable groups in society.

Guppy restricted his study to names which appeared in a proportion of 7:10,000 or higher and he found the name as Barratt, Barrett and Barritt:

> Buckinghamshire – 18
> Cambridgeshire – 24
> Cheshire – 22
> Cornwall – 9
> Devon – 8

Dorset – 21
Essex – 27
Gloucestershire – 14
Lincolnshire – 8
Norfolk – 29
Northamptonshire – 25
Nottinghamshire – 20
Oxfordshire – 20
Yorkshire, West Riding – 20

Guppy found that the usual form of the surname was Barrett, but that Cheshire, Nottinghamshire, Lincolnshire and in parts of Northamptonshire, Barratt was more common. He also found the variant Barritt in Essex, which, in that county, was the most common form of the name. Like Lower and George Redmonds, he assumed that the name originated as a personal one.

There is no entry for the surname Barrett *etc* in George F Black's *The Surnames of Scotland* (New York, 1946), or in T J Morgan and Prys Morgan's *Welsh Surnames* (1985). Edward MacLysaght's *The Surnames of Ireland* (1973) and his *Guide to Irish Surnames* (1965) suggest that the surname arrived in Ireland in the late twelfth century and gave rise to two Irish forms of the name:

Barrett
Baróid in Munster, *Bairèid* in Connacht. These families, which were branches of the same stock, came with the Anglo-Norman invasion and became completely hibernicized.

These two Irish variants also found their way by the early sixteenth century to the Isle of Man, as shown by a study of *The Personal Names of the Isle of Man* by J J Kneen (1937), who like other early scholars found no difficulty in treating the Domesday 'Baret/Bared' and the Germanic personal names as part of the same group:

Barrett VII

Barett, Barrett *Libri Assed* (from 1515 onwards) (Manx Record Office) 7, II 1515; Baret *Libri Episcop* (Manx Record Office) 10 B 1580;Cf. Ir[ish]

Bared, Baret, Barrett

Bared and Baret occur in [the] Domesday Book as names of persons holding land in the time of Edward the Confessor. The name is, therefore, probably A[nglo]-S[axon]. The name also occurs as a derivative from 'Baraud', a N[orman] form of the Teut[onic] Berwald (bear-forest). There were two distinct families in Ireland from whence our M[an]x name probably came. The former settle in Tirawley and the latter in Cork.

J Barret, preacher of the Gospel, d[ied] 1795

Bardsley (1901), whose entry on the origins of the surname has been discussed above, noted that the surname Barrett *etc* appeared in a London commercial directory from 1890 and a Philadelphia directory from 1885 in the following numbers:

Name: (Nos signify London; then Philadelphia)
Barrat: 9; 1
Barratt: 22; 2
Baret: 1; 0
Barett: 87; 160
Berrett: 1; 0
Berret: 0; 2

This shows that by far the largest group were using the variant Barett in both London and Philadelphia at the end of the nineteenth century.

Many of the sources available for charting surname distribution through the centuries are necessarily confined to the wealthier sectors of the population: in general, nobody wanted to know the names of the poor but the names of those with money or land were naturally of interest to the authorities. However, one source that covers the whole of the social spectrum is provided by English parish registers, the earliest of which began in 1538 following a mandate that all parish priests should keep a weekly record of all baptisms, marriages and burials that took place in their parish.

In 1910, F K and S Hitching carried out a survey of a cross section of parish registers for the years 1601 and 1602; incidences of a particular surname are noted by parish and county, although with no indication of numbers of references.

1601
Barret
Derby St Alkmund, Derbyshire
St Mary Woolnoth, London
St Mary's Harrow, Middlesex
Moulton, Northamptonshire
Bardwell, Suffolk
Skipton in Craven, Yorkshire

Barrett
Barnstaple, Devon

Barrette
Dalston, Cumberland

1602
Barrat
Harrow, Middlesex

Barret
St Tudy, Cornwall
Cheltenham, Gloucestershire
St Botolph, Bishopsgate, London
Moulton, Northamptonshire

Barrett
Barnstaple, Devon
St Dionis, Backchurch, London
Stepney, St Dunstan, Middlesex
Pontesbury, Shropshire

Barrit
Rylstone, Yorkshire

Barret(t) was fairly widely spread throughout England at the beginning of the seventeenth century but with no entries from Kent, East Anglia or Lincolnshire. The rarer form Barrette was found in Cumbria; Barrit appeared in north Yorkshire and Barrat in Middlesex.

A useful guide to the distribution of surnames for the sixteenth, seventeenth and eighteenth centuries in England is provided by the indexes to wills proved, and administrations granted, at the Prerogative Court of (the Archbishop of) Canterbury, in London, which had superior jurisdiction over local ecclesiastical courts where wills were proved until 1858. The PCC thus provides a national index, although it is not a completely representative one, as testators whose wills were proved in the PCC were mostly among the wealthier members of society, and a disproportionate number of them were from London or Middlesex.

A search of the printed indexes for the years 1558 to 1583; 1584 to 1604; 1605 to 1619; 1620 to 1629; 1653 to 1656; 1657 to 1660; 1661 to 1670; 1671 to 1675; 1676 to 1685; 1686 to 1693; 1694 to 1700; 1701 to 1749; and 1750 to 1800 found the following Barrett *etc* entries:

1558-1599
Berkshire: Barrett (2)
Cambridgeshire: Barrett (4); Barritt (1)
Cornwall: Barrett (1)
Derbyshire: Barrett (1)
Devon: Barrett (1)
Dorset: Barrett (1)
Essex: Barrett (2)
Hampshire: Barrett (2)
Hertfordshire: Barret (1); Barrett (1)
London: Barret (1); Barrett (2)
Montgomeryshire: Barrett (1)
Norfolk: Barrett (1)
Nottinghamshire: Barrett (1)
Oxfordshire: Barrett (1)
Pts: Barrett (1)
Salop: Barrett (2)
Somerset: Barrett (1)
Suffolk: Barret (1); Barrett (4)
Surrey: Barrat (1); Barrett (1)

Warwickshire: Barrett (1)
Wiltshire: Barret (1)

The name had spread throughout a large part of England and Wales by the end of the sixteenth century; the most common variant found at this time was Barrett. We have one example of a Barrett testator dying overseas: 'Pts' (*in partibus transmarinus*).

Seventeenth Century
Bedfordshire: Barrett (1)
Berkshire: Barret (1); Barrett (3)
Buckinghamshire: Barret (1); Barrett (2)
Cambridgeshire: Barrett (2)
Carmarthenshire: Barrett (1)
Cheshire: Barrett (1)
Cornwall: Barrett (1)
Devon: Barret (1); Barrett (2)
Dorset: Barrett (1)
Essex: Barret (3); Barrett (5)
Gloucestershire: Barratt (1); Barret (1); Barrett (2)
Herefordshire: Barrett (2)
Hertfordshire: Barrett (1)
Kent: Barrett (2)
Leicestershire: Barrett (2)
London: Barratt (3); Baret (1); Barrett (20)
Middlesex: Barratt (2); Barrett (18); Barritt (1)
Monmouthshire: Barret (1)
Montgomeryshire: Barret (1)
Norfolk: Barret (3); Barrett (4); Barritt (1)
Northamptonshire: Barrett (5); Barritt (1)
Nottinghamshire: Barratt (1); Barrett (1)
Oxfordshire: Barrett (2)
Pts: Barratt (1); Barret (1); Barrett (7)
Salop: Barrat (1); Barret (1); Barrett (1)

Somerset: Barrat (1); Barratt (3); Barret (1); Barrett (4)
Staffordshire: Barret (1)
Suffolk: Barret (1); Barrett (3)
Surrey: Barratt (1); Barret (1); Barrett (9)
Sussex: Barrett (1)
Warwickshire: Barrett (3)
Wiltshire: Barrat (1); Barratt (1); Barret (2); Barrett (1)
Worcestershire: Barrett (1)
Yorkshire: Barritt (1)

As might be expected, many of the testators using the PCC during the seventeenth century were mariners and again the most commonly used form was Barrett. We have examples of the name as Barritt and evidence of the name being used as an alias (John Barrett of HMS *Guernsey* in 1692 was also known as John Lash) and fewer examples of the name as Baret compared to the previous period; signifying, perhaps, that the spelling of the name was settling into the form Barrett.

1700-1749
Berkshire: Barrett (5)
Buckinghamshire: Barrett (1)
Cornwall: Barrett (1)
Devon: Barrett (3)
Dorset: Barrett (2)
Essex: Barret (1); Barrett (2)
Gloucestershire: Barret (1); Barrett (1)
Hampshire: Barrett (2)
Kent: Barrett (8)
London: Barret (1); Barrett (11)
Middlesex: Barret (6); Barrett (27)
Montgomeryshire: Barret (1)
Oxfordshire: Barret (1); Barrett (7)

Pts: Barratt (1); Barret (2); Barrett (42)
Salop: Barrett (1)
Shropshire: Barret (1); Barrett (4)
Somerset: Barrett (2)
Suffolk: Barret (1)
Surrey: Barrett (15)
Sussex: Barrett (1)
Wiltshire: Barrett (5)

As we can see by the beginning of the eighteenth century, Barrett was the dominant form of the name, with a few examples of the variant Barret.

1750-1800
Bedfordshire: Barratt (1)
Berkshire: Barret (1); Barrett (5)
Buckinghamshire: Barratt (1); Barrett (1)
Cornwall: Barrett (1)
Devon: Barrett (1)
Dorset: Barrett (1)
Essex: Barratt (3); Barret (1); Barrett (2)
Gloucestershire: Barratt (4); Barrett (2)
Hampshire: Barratt (1); Barrett (2)
Herefordshire: Barrett (1)
Hertfordshire: Barrett (1)
Kent: Barratt (2); Barret (1); Barrett (6)
Lincolnshire: Barrett (1)
London: Barrat (1); Barratt (2); Barrett (12); Barrit (1);
    Barritt (2)
Middlesex: Baratt (1); Barratt (8); Barrett (26); Barrit (1);
    Barritt (3)
Norfolk: Baret (2)
Northamptonshire: Barrett (1)
Oxfordshire: Barrett (1)

Pts: Barrat (2); Barratt (8); Barret (4); Barrett (43);
   Barrit (1); Barritt (2)
Salop: Barrett (2)
Somerset: Barrett (3)
Staffordshire: Barrett (5)
Suffolk: Barrett (2)
Surrey: Barratt (2); Barrett (10)
Sussex: Barrett (2)
Warwickshire: Barratt (3); Barrett (1)
Wiltshire: Barratt (2); Barrett (2)
Worcestershire: Barrett (1)

A large number of Barrett *etc* testators during the latter half of the eighteenth century died overseas, 43 of them using the form Barrett. Middlesex has the next largest number, with 26; again the most common form used is Barrett.

For the nineteenth century, H B Guppy's survey has been mentioned above. Another important Victorian source is the *Return of Owners of Land* of 1873, sometimes known as the Modern Domesday Book. This source lists, county by county, every owner of an acre of land or more, with their residence (not necessarily the address of their property) and the acreage of their holding.

Return of Owners of Land
Bedfordshire – Barrett (1)
Berkshire – Barratt (1), Barrett (3)
Buckinghamshire – Barratt (3), Barrett (3)
Cambridgeshire – Barratt (6), Barrett (3)
Carmarthenshire – Barratt (1), Barrett (1)
Cheshire – Barratt (10), Barrett (1)
Cornwall – Barrett (11)

Cumberland – Barratt (3), Barrett (1)
Derbyshire – Barratt (2)
Devon – Barratt (3), Barrett (3)
Dorset – Barratt (3), Barrett (1)
Essex – Barrett (3), Barritt (3), Barritts (1)
Glamorganshire – Barret (1)
Gloucestershire – Barette (1), Barratt (1), Barrett (10)
Hampshire – Barratt (1), Barrett (7)
Herefordshire – Barrett (6)
Huntingdonshire – Barrett (1)
Kent – Barrett (3)
Lancashire – Barratt (4), Barrett (4), Barritt (1)
Leicestershire – Barratt (2)
Lincolnshire – Barratt (8), Barrett (8)
Middlesex –Barrett (1)
Montgomeryshire – Barrett (1)
Norfolk – Barrett (13)
Northamptonshire – Barratt (1), Barrett (2), Barritt (2)
Nottinghamshire – Barratt (2)
Oxfordshire – Barrett (2)
Salop – Barrett (3)
Somerset – Barrett (7)
Staffordshire – Barratt (3)
Suffolk – Barrett (3), Barritt (1)
Surrey – Barrett (7)
Sussex – Barrett (2)
Warwickshire – Barratt (2), Barret (1), Barrett (1)
Westmorland – Barratt (1), Barretts (1)
Wiltshire – Barrett (6)
Worcestershire – Barrett (2)
Yorkshire, East Riding – Barratt (1), Barrett (4)
Yorkshire, West Riding – Barratt (2), Barrett (15),
    Barritt (2)

Nearly every county in England had a least one landowner named Barrett *etc.* We also noted that a Baron Henry Barretto of London owned land in several counties; this is probably a cognate form of the surname.

The first decennial census return in England, Scotland and Wales was taken in 1801, but personal information was only recorded from 1841 onwards. The latest return currently open to public inspection is that of 1911 and there are now national indexes to the returns from 1841 onwards, although these indexes are not wholly reliable. Using these indexes, we found the following numbers for Barrett, Barret, Barrat, Barratt, Barritt and Barrott, in England, Scotland and Wales:

> **6 June 1841** – Barrett (9598); Barret (968); Barrat (350); Barratt (3625); Barritt (603); Barrott (368)
>
> **30 March 1851** – Barrett (10,924); Barret (967); Barrat (323); Barratt (3906); Barritt (724); Barrott (531)
>
> **7 April 1861** – Barrett (10,988); Barret (947); Barrat (277); Barratt (2640); Barritt (951); Barrott (716)
>
> **2 April 1871** – Barrett (17,006); Barret (909); Barrat (254); Barratt (5198); Barritt (880); Barrott (366)
>
> **3 April 1881** – Barrett (20,068); Barret (834); Barrat (184); Barratt (6067); Barritt (788); Barrott (196)
>
> **5 April 1891** – Barrett (20,698); Barret (685); Barrat (166); Barratt (5961); Barritt (1059); Barrott (423)
>
> **31 March 1901** – Barrett (25,024); Barret (480); Barrat (143); Barratt (7443); Barritt (1127); Barrott (258)
>
> **2 April 1911** – Barrett (27,149); Barret (400); Barrat (194); Barratt (7833); Barritt (1139); Barrott (336)

As expected, Barrett is the most widely found form with Barratt being the second most prevalent. Like the

21

population generally, the numbers for Barrett increase dramatically between 1861 and 1871 and continue to increase thereafter. None of the variants of this surname reaches similar numbers and the form Barret declines throughout the records, with some Barrets presumably becoming Barretts.

Famous Bearers of the Name

The *Dictionary of National Biography* for the British Isles has numerous entries for people named Barrett *etc*:

Eaton Stannard Barrett (1786-1820) – author and poet

Elizabeth Barrett Browning (1806-1861) – poet

George Barret the elder (circa 1728-1784) – landscape painter and one of the original members of the Royal Academy

George Barret the younger (died 1842) – landscape painter and son of the above

George Barrett (1752-1821) – actuary

John Barret DD (died 1563) – Carmelite friar later protestant clergyman

John Barret or Barrett (died circa 1580) – lexicographer

John Barrett (died 1810) – Royal Navy Captain

John Barrett DD (1753-1821) – vice-provost and professor of oriental languages at Trinity College, Dublin

John Barret (1631-1713) – non-conformist divine

Joseph Barret (1665-1699) – theological writer and son of the above

Lucas Barrett (1837-1862) – geologist and naturalist

Patrick Barret (died 1415) – ecclesiastic, judge and bishop

Richard Barret DD (died 1599) – catholic divine

Robert Barret (fl 1600) – military and poetical writer

Stephen Barrett (1718-1801) – classical teacher and author

Thomas Barritt (1743-1820) – antiquary

William Barret (died 1584) – British Consul at Aleppo

William Barret (fl 1595) – divine

William Barrett (1733-1789) – surgeon and antiquary
(William Henry) Wilson Barrett (1846-1904) – actor,
   playwright and manager of Lyric Theatre and Globe
   Theatre, London

The name Barrett-Lennard appears in the baronetage: Sir Peter John Barrett-Lennard (born 1942) is the 7th Baronet of Belhus.

There are a great many coats of arms listed in Burke's *General Armory* granted to men of the name Barrett *etc*:

Baret Gules on a chief indented argent three escallops of the first (another within a bordure azure)
Barett Gules a chief indented argent
Barett Argent a cross gules five ducks of the field. Crest – A demi leopard guarding proper
Barett Argent a bend azure between three lozenge buckles gules tongues in fesse an annulet for difference
Barett Azure a fesse dancettée or, in chief three mullets pierced argent
Barratt Argent three lozenge buckles in bend gules. Crest – A galley, her oars in saltire sable flags gules
Barrett (Cambridge) – Argent a chevron engrossed between three bears passant sable muzzled or. Crest – A griffin sergeant reguard or, beak, legs and wings gules
Barrett (Dorsetshire and Ealing, county Middlesex) – Sable a chevron between three hawks' heads or
Barrett (Bellhouse, Aveley, county Essex) – Argent and gules barry of four counterchanged. Crest – A hydra with seven heads wings endorsed vert scaled or
Barrett (Essex) – Per pale argent and gules four bars counterchanged (another, of Kent, six)

24

Barrett (Winsole, county Leicester, Herald's Visitation 1619) – Per pale argent and gules a fesse counterchanged

Barrett (Herefordshire) – Gules on a chief indented argent three escallops of the field (another sable). Crest – A lion rampant or, holding between his fore feet an escallop sable

Barrett (Milton House, county Berkshire) – Gules on a chief indented argent three escallops of the first quartering Belsour. Crest – A wyvern wings erect or, collared and chained azure. Motto – *Honor virtus probitas*

Barrett (Ireland) – Per Pale argent and gules twelve barrulets counterchanged

Barrett (Lee Priory, county Kent) – Or on a chevron between three mullets sable as many lions passant guarding argent (sometimes or). Crest – A lion couchant argent the dexter paw resting upon a mullet sable

Barrett (Perry Court, county Kent) – Argent a fesse dancettée gules in chief three mullets sable

Barrett (London, 1383) – Gules a chief indented argent a bordure azure

Barrett (London, granted 1773) – Azure two barrulets or, between three doves proper

Barrett (Castle Barrett, county Cork, granted 1689) – Per pale argent and gules barry of seven counterchanged a canton of the second charged with a rose imperially ensigned or. Crest – A heart or between two wings conjoined sable semée of étoiles gold. Motto – In uprightness God will support us

Barrett (Shortney, county Nottinghamshire) – Gules on a fesse cottised between three spear heads argent as many mullets of the field. Crest – A nag's head erased per pale gules and azure gorged with two bars argent

Barrett (Suffolk) – Argent a bend azure between three square buckles gules. Crest – A helmet argent garnished and plumed with feathers or. Another Crest – a demi greyhound argent collared and lined sable

Barrett (Suffolk) – Argent on a bend azure between three lozenge buckles the tongues fesseways gules an annulet or

Barrett (Suffolk) – A fesse between three mullets sable

Barrett (Warwickshire) – Or a chevron engrossed gules between three bears' heads sable muzzled or. Crest – A griffin segreant reguard gules wings elevated or

Barrett (Tregarden, or Tregarne, county Cornwall) – Same arms field argent

Barrett (funeral entry, Ireland) – Azure on a chevron argent between three trefoils slipped ermine three lions rampant sable

Barrett Azure a fesse indented in chief three mullets argent

Barrett (Ireland) – Argent two pallets gules

Barrett (Ireland) – Azure a fesse nebulae and in chief three mullets argent

Barrett Sable three falcons' heads erased or

Barrett Or a cross sable over all a bendlet gules

Barrett Gules on a saltire or five swans sable

Barrett Per pale argent and gules a fesse counterchanged

Barrett Gules on a chief indented argent three martlets sable

Barrett Azure on a chief indented argent three escallops sable

Barrett Gules on a chief indented or three escallops sable

Barrett Argent a fesse sable in chief three mullets of the second

Barrett A fesse dancettée or in chief three mullets argent

Barrett Argent a fesse between three estoiles gules

Barrett Per fesse indented argent and gules a bordure azure

Barrett (granted to Leonard Barrett of Defonden by Cooke, Clarencieux 1575) Argent a chevron engrossed gules between three bears passant sable muzzled or

Barrett (Exeter) Chequy argent and sable

Barrett Argent semy of crosses crosslet a lion rampant gules crowned or. Sire Steven Barret

Barrette (Dorset) Sable a chevron argent between three hawks' heads erased or

Barrette (London) Erminois three bars gules on a canton argent a female bust couped at the shoulders proper

Barritt (Jamaica) Azure on a chevron ermine between three griffins' heads erased or two serpents in saltire as part of a caduceus proper. Crest – A talbot's head per fesse argent and ermine collared or cared sable

Barrett-Lennard (Belhus, county Essex, Bart) – Quarterly, 1st and 4th or on a fesse gules three fleurs-de-lis of the first for Lennard; 2nd and 3rd per pale argent and gules barry of four counterchanged for Barrett all within a bordure wavy sable. Crest – Out of a ducal coronet or an Irish Wolf-dog's head per fesse argent and ermine charged with an escallop barways nebulée gules and sable. Motto – *La loi le veut, et moi ni mot; Pour bien desirer*; and *La bondad para la medra*

Printed Genealogies

The following printed genealogies for Barrett (*etc*) families are listed in standard bibliographies:

Barratt
Burke's *Landed Gentry* 1937, 1969

Baret, Barett, Barret, Barrett,
Rev Alfred Suckling LLB, *The History and Antiquities of the County of Suffolk* (London, 1846-8)
Burke's *Dormant & Extinct Peerages*
Burke's *Extinct & Dormant Baronetcies*
Sir Thomas Phillipps Bart, Ed., *The Cambridge Visitations by Henry St George 1619* (MSS, 1840)
Sir Nicholas Harris Nicholas Ed, *Visitation of Cornwall made in the year 1620 by W Camden and St George* (foolscap folio, ?1838)
Robert Thoroton, *The Antiquities of Nottinghamshire* (London, 1677)
Sir Thomas Phillipps Bart, *Visitatio Heradlica Comitatus Wiltoniæ, Ann 1623* (privately printed, 1828)
Sir Samuel Rush Meyrick Ed, *Heraldic Visitations of Wales and part of the Marches, between the years 1586 and 1613 by Lewys Dwnn* (Llandovery, 1846)
Burke's *Landed Gentry* 1860, 1863, 1937, 1952, 1965, 1969
Burke's *Distinguished Families of the USA*
John Nichols FSA, *The History and Antiquities of the County of Leicester* (London, 1795-1807)
Sir Richard Colt Hoare Bart, *The History of Modern Wiltshire* (London, 1822-1843)

John Philipps Allen Lloyd Phillipps Esq of Dale Castle, Pembrokeshire, *Pedigrees of Caermarthenshire, Cardiganshire and Pembrokeshire in continuation of Lewis Dwnn, to about the years 1700-10* (privately printed by Sir Thomas Phillipps Bart, 1859)

J Marks, *The Family of the Barrett* (New York, 1938)

Kent Visitations 1663 (Harleian Society) liv, 9

Norfolk Visitations 1664 (Harleian Society) lxxxv, 15

Yorkshire Pedigrees (Harleian Society) xciv, 42

Miscellanea Genealogica et Heraldica 5th series, vi

The Marquis of Ruvigny and Raineval, *The Plantagenet Roll of the Blood Royal, the Mortimer Percy volume* (1911)

J J Muskett, *Suffolk Manorial Families* (1894-1914) ii

Norfolk Archaeology: Transactions of the Norfolk and Norwich Archaeological Society xv

Essex Review xv

Transactions of the Lancashire & Cheshire Antiquarian Society iii

P Millican, *History of Horstead and Stannighall* (1937)

Who's Who in the Theatre 1936

Journal of the Cork Historical and Archaeological Society 2nd series xvi

J G White, *Historical and Topographical Notes etc on Buttevant* (CHS, 1905-1916) i

Morant's *Essex*

Hasted's *Kent*

Maclean's *History of Trigg Minor*

O'Hart's *Irish Pedigrees*

Wood's *Douglas's Peerage of Scotland*

Metcalfe's *Visitations of Suffolk*

G W Marshall ed, *Visitations of Wiltshire*

Archaeologia Cantiana xiv

Carthew's *Hundred of Launditch* part iii

G T Clark, *Genealogies of Morgan and Glamorgan*

New England Register xlii

Howard's *Visitation of England and Wales*

Barrett-Lennard

John Burke & John Bernard Burke, *The Royal Families of England, Scotland and Wales with their descendants* (London, 1851)

T B Lennard, *An Account of the Families of Lennard and Barrett* (1908)

The Marquis of Ruvigny and Raineval, *The Plantagenet Roll of the Blood Royal, the Mortimer Percy volume* (1911)

W Rye, *Norfolk Families* (1915)

Berry's *Essex Genealogies*

Shirley, *History of the County of Monaghan*

Edmondson's *Baronagium Genealogicum*

Betham's *Baronetage* v

Barritt

Jamaica Pedigrees

Jewitt's *Reliquary* is, xiii

Summary

To conclude, the name Barrett is of uncertain and controversial origin: it has been described variously by scholars as 'great' and 'difficult'. By the nineteenth century the dominant form was Barrett, which has spread throughout the whole of England and Wales; and the name has evolved separately from medieval origins in Ireland and the Isle of Man.

Sources Consulted

P H Reaney, *The Origins of English Surnames* (London: Routledge & Kegan Paul 1967)

P H Reaney & R M Wilson, *A Dictionary of British Surnames* (London: Oxford University Press, 3rd edition 1995)

P H Reaney, *A Dictionary of British Surnames* (London: Routledge & Kegan Paul, 2nd edition 1976)

P Hanks & F Hodges, *A Dictionary of Surnames* (Oxford University Press 1988)

M A Lower, *Patronymica Brittanica* (London 1860)

C W Bardsley, *Dictionary of English and Welsh Surnames* (1901: reprinted, Baltimore: Genealogical Publishing Co. 1967)

C L'Estrange Ewen, *Guide to the Origin of British Surnames* (London: John Gifford 1938)

H B Guppy, *Homes of Family Names in Great Britain* (London 1890)

Ernest Weekley, *The Romance of Names* (London: John Murray, 2nd edition 1917)

Ernest Weekley, *Surnames* (London: John Murray 1917)

George F Black, *The Surnames of Scotland* (New York Public Library 1946)

Edward McLysaght, *The Surnames of Ireland* (Dublin: Irish University Press 1977)

T J & Prys Morgan, *Welsh Surnames* (Cardiff: University of Wales Press 1985)

F K & S Hitching, *References to English Surnames in 1601* (Walton on Thames: Bernau 1910)

F K & S Hitching, *References to English Surnames in 1602* (Walton on Thames: Bernau 1911)

Debrett's People of Today (Debrett's Peerage Limited 1996)

The Dictionary of National Biography: Index & Epitome (London 1906)

The Concise Dictionary of National Biography, 1901-1950 (Oxford 1961)

Burke's Family Index (London: Burke's Peerage Limited 1976)

H R Moulton, *Palaeography, Genealogy & Topography* (1930)

Prerogative Court of Canterbury Wills (online index)

Online index to England, Scotland and Wales census returns 1841-1911

G W Marshall, *The Genealogist's Guide* (1903; reprinted, Baltimore: GPC 1973)

J B Whitmore, *A Genealogical Guide* (London 1953)

Charles Bridge, *An Index to Pedigrees* (London 1867)

Geoffrey B Barrow, *The Genealogist's Guide* (London: Research Publishing Co. 1977)

Sir Bernard Burke, *The General Armory* (London 1884)

C R Humphrey-Smith ed., *Burke's General Armory Volume II*, (Tabard Press 1973)

The Return of Owners of Land (1873)

Eilert Ekwall, *The Oxford Dictionary of English Place Names* (4th edition: Oxford 1960)

E G Withycombe, *The Oxford Dictionary of English Christian Names* (Oxford: Clarendon Press, 2nd edition 1950)

W J Hardy & W Page, *A Calendar to the Feet of Fines for London and Middlesex:* Vol 1 Richard I- Richard III (1189-1485) (London 1892)

Richard McKinley, *The Surnames of Oxford* (Leopards Head Press, 1977)

Richard McKinley, *The Surnames of Sussex* (Leopards Head Press, 1988)

Richard McKinley, *The Surnames of Lancashire* (Leopards Head Press, 1981)

Richard McKinley, *The Surnames of Norfolk and Suffolk* (Phillimore 1975)

George Redmonds, *The Surnames of Yorkshire West Riding* (Phillimore 1973)

Mr Avenell, *The Norman People* (London 1874)

J J Kneen, *The Personal Names of the Isle of Man* (Oxford 1937)

L G Pine, *They Came with the Conqueror* (Evans 1954)

www.ingramcontent.com/pod-product-compliance
Lightning Source LLC
Chambersburg PA
CBHW070843310526
45793CB00011B/525